Edward Everett, Charles Stewart, Joseph Holt

Letters of the Commodore Charles Stewart on the present

crisis

Edward Everett, Charles Stewart, Joseph Holt

Letters of the Commodore Charles Stewart on the present crisis

ISBN/EAN: 9783337018085

Printed in Europe, USA, Canada, Australia, Japan

Cover: Foto ©ninafisch / pixelio.de

More available books at **www.hansebooks.com**

LETTERS

OF THE

HON. JOSEPH HOLT,

THE

HON. EDWARD EVERETT,

AND

COMMODORE CHARLES STEWART,

ON THE

PRESENT CRISIS.

PHILADELPHIA:

WILLIAM S. & ALFRED MARTIEN,

No. 606 Chestnut Street.

1861.

LETTERS

OF THE

HON. JOSEPH HOLT,

THE

HON. EDWARD EVERETT,

AND

COMMODORE CHARLES STEWART,

ON THE

PRESENT CRISIS.

PHILADELPHIA:

WILLIAM S. & ALFRED MARTIEN,

No. 606 Chestnut Street.

1861.

PREFATORY NOTE.

MR. HOLT is already well known to the country as the Post-Master General, and subsequently, for a few weeks, the Secretary of War under President Buchanan. The ability and efficiency with which he administered these trusts, commanded the general approval of the country; while the personal and official corruption by which he was surrounded, brought into bolder relief his own spotless integrity. It was quite in keeping with the antecedents of such a man, that he should write the Letter here reprinted. He saw his native State dallying with the demon of secession—as Satan beguiled our first mother.

> "Oft he bowed
> His turret-crest, and sleek enamelled neck,
> Fawning; and licked the ground whereon she trod."

This was not a sight for a true patriot to see unmoved; and he addressed the following Letter to the "People of Kentucky." The special design of the appeal, is to keep that State from sliding into the abyss before her. But in aiming at this object, he has discussed the whole subject of the pending contest with masterly ability. He traces the secession movement to its true sources; lays bare the sordid motives of the Confederate leaders; and shows that the treason which is now making war against our just and beneficent Government, has been covertly plotting the overthrow of the Union for many years.

His views on these points are confirmed by the other Letters herewith published. MR. EVERETT states it, as of his personal knowledge, that "leading Southern politicians had for thirty years been resolved to break up the Union," whenever the sceptre departed from their hands. And the venerable COMMODORE STEWART traces the roots of this foul scheme back as far as 1812. These testimonies, in connection with the recent letter of Mr. Russell to the *London Times*, seem to justify the presumption, that the State of South Carolina was *never* loyal to the Union; that, however it may have been with the mass of her people, she had nursed *ab initio* a nest of traitors, who have persistently cherished the purpose to destroy the Government whenever they could no longer control it.

These developments are of great moment in their bearing upon the present conflict; and they will not be lost sight of in the future adjustment of this quarrel.

The three Letters contained in this pamphlet are of too much value to be consigned merely to the fugitive columns of a newspaper. The Publisher feels that he is doing the country a good service, by presenting them in a form suitable for preservation and reference. Without specifying other topics which are worthy of notice, he may be allowed to direct particular attention to the paragraph of Mr. EVERETT's admirable Letter (pp. 38, 39) on the plausible claim of the South, "simply to be let alone."

PHILADELPHIA, June 25, 1861.

LETTER OF THE HON. J. HOLT.

———◆◆◆———

J. F. SPEED, Esq.

WASHINGTON, Friday, *May* 31, 1861.

My Dear Sir—The recent overwhelming vote in favour of the Union in Kentucky has afforded unspeakable gratification to all true men throughout the country. That vote indicates that the people of that gallant State have been neither seduced by the arts nor terrified by the menaces of the revolutionists in their midst, and that it is their fixed purpose to remain faithful to a Government which, for nearly seventy years, has remained faithful to them. Still it cannot be denied that there is in the bosom of that State a band of agitators, who, though few in number, are yet powerful from the public confidence they have enjoyed, and who have been, and doubtless will continue to be, unceasing in their endeavour to force Kentucky to unite her fortunes with those of the rebel Confederacy of the South. In view of this and of the well-known fact that several of the seceded States have by fraud and violence been driven to occupy their present false and fatal position, I cannot, even with the encouragement of her late vote before me, look upon the

A*

political future of our native State without a painful
solicitude. Never have the safety and honour of her
people required the exercise of so much vigilance and of
so much courage on their part. If true to themselves,
the Stars and Stripes, which, like angels' wings, have so
long guarded their homes from every oppression, will still
be theirs; but if, chasing the dreams of men's ambition,
they shall prove false, the blackness of darkness can but
faintly predict the gloom that awaits them. The Legislature, it seems, has determined by resolution that the
State, pending the present unhappy war, shall occupy
neutral ground. *I must say, in all frankness, and without desiring to reflect upon the course or sentiments of
any, that, in this struggle for the existence of our Government, I can neither practise nor profess nor feel neutral-
ity. I would as soon think of being neutral in a contest
between an officer of justice and an incendiary arrested in
an attempt to fire the dwelling over my head; for the
Government whose overthrow is sought, is for me the shelter
not only of home, kindred and friends, but of every earthly
blessing which I can hope to enjoy on this side of the grave.*
If, however, from a natural horror of fratricidal strife, or
from her intimate social and business relations with the
South, Kentucky shall determine to maintain the neutral
attitude assumed for her by her Legislature, her position
will still be an honourable one, though falling far short of
that full measure of loyalty which her history has so con-
stantly illustrated. Her Executive, ignoring, as I am
happy to believe, alike the popular and legislative sentiment of the State, has, by proclamation, forbidden the
Government of the United States from marching troops
across her territory. This is in no sense a neutral step,

but one of aggressive hostility. The troops of the Federal Government have as clear a constitutional right to pass over the soil of Kentucky as they have to march along the streets of Washington; and could this prohibition be effective, it would not only be a violation of the fundamental law, but would, in all its tendencies, be directly in advancement of the revolution, and might, in an emergency easily imagined, compromise the highest national interests. I was rejoiced that the Legislature so promptly refused to endorse this proclamation as expressive of the true policy of the State. But I turn away from even this to the ballot-box, and find an abounding consolation in the conviction it inspires, that the popular heart of Kentucky, in its devotion to the Union, is far in advance alike of legislative resolve and of Executive proclamation.

But as it is well understood that the late popular demonstration has rather scotched than killed rebellion in Kentucky, I propose inquiring, as briefly as practicable, whether, in the recent action or present declared policy of the Administration, or in the history of the pending revolution, or in the objects it seeks to accomplish, or in the results which must follow from it, if successful, there can be discovered any reasons why that State should sever the ties that unite her with a Confederacy in whose councils and upon whose battle-fields she has won so much fame, and under whose protection she has enjoyed so much prosperity.

For more than a month after the inauguration of President LINCOLN, the manifestations seemed unequivocal that his Administration would seek a peaceful solution of our unhappy political troubles, and would look to time and amendments to the Federal Constitution, adopted in

accordance with its provisions, to bring back the revolted
States to their allegiance. So marked was the effect of
these manifestations in tranquilizing the Border States
and in reassuring their loyalty, that the conspirators who.
had set this revolution on foot took the alarm. *While
affecting to despise these States as not sufficiently intensi-
fied in their devotion to African servitude, they knew they
could never succeed in their treasonable enterprise without
their support. Hence it was resolved to precipitate a
collision of arms with the Federal authorities, in the hope
that under the panic and exasperation incident to the
commencement of a civil war, the Border States, following
the natural bent of their sympathies, would array themselves against the Government.* Fort Sumter, occupied
by a feeble garrison, and girdled by powerful if not
impregnable batteries, afforded convenient means for
accomplishing their purpose, and for testing also their
favorite theory, that blood was needed to cement the new
Confederacy. Its provisions were exhausted, and the
request made by the President, in the interests of peace
and humanity, for the privilege of replenishing its stores,
had been refused. The Confederate authorities were
aware—for so the gallant commander of the fort had
declared to them—that in two days a capitulation from
starvation must take place. A peaceful surrender, however, would not have subserved their aims. They sought
the clash of arms and the effusion of blood as an instrumentality for impressing the Border States, and they
sought the humiliation of the Government and the dis-
honour of its flag as a means of giving prestige to their
own cause. The result is known. Without the slightest
provocation, a heavy cannonade was opened upon the

fort, and borne by its helpless garrison for hours without reply; and when, in the progress of the bombardment, the fortification became wrapped in flames, the besieging batteries, in violation of the usages of civilized warfare, instead of relaxing or suspending, redoubled their fires. *A more wanton or wicked war was never commenced on any Government whose history has been written.* Cotemporary with and following the fall of Sumter, the siege of Fort Pickens was and still is actively pressed; the property of the United States Government continued to be seized wherever found, and its troops, by fraud or force, captured in the State of Texas, in violation of a solemn compact with its authorities that they should be permitted to embark without molestation. This was the requital which the Lone Star State made to brave men, who, through long years of peril and privation, had guarded its frontiers against the incursions of the savages. In the midst of the most active and extended warlike preparations in the South, the announcement was made by the Secretary of War of the seceded States, and echoed with taunts and insolent bravadoes by the Southern press, that Washington City was to be invaded and captured, and that the flag of the Confederate States would soon float over the dome of its capitol. Soon thereafter there followed an invitation to all the world—embracing necessarily the outcasts and desperadoes of every sea—to accept letters of marque and reprisal, to prey upon the rich and unprotected commerce of the United States.

In view of these events and threatenings, what was the duty of the Chief Magistrate of the Republic? He might have taken counsel of the revolutionists and trembled under their menaces; he might, upon the fall of Sumter, have directed that Fort Pickens should be surrendered without firing a gun in its defence, and proceeding yet further, and meeting fully the requirements of the "let us alone" policy insisted on in the South, he might have ordered that the Stars and Stripes should be laid in the dust in the presence of every bit of rebel bunting that might appear. *But he did none of these things, nor could he have done them without forfeiting his oath and betraying the most sublime trust that has ever been confided to the hands of man.* With a heroic fidelity to his constitutional obligations, feeling justly that these obligations charged him with the protection of the Republic and its Capital against the assaults alike of foreign and domestic enemies, he threw himself on the loyalty of the country for support in the struggle upon which he was about to enter, and nobly has that appeal been responded to. States containing an aggregate population of nineteen millions have answered to the appeal as with the voice of one man, offering soldiers without number, and treasure without limitation for the service of the Government. In these States, fifteen hundred thousand freemen cast their votes in favour of candidates supporting the rights of the South, at the last Presidential election, and yet everywhere, alike in popular assembles and upon the tented field, this million and a half of voters are found yielding to none in the zeal with which they rally to their country's flag. They are not less the friends of the South than before; but they realize that the question now presented is not one of administrative policy, or of the claims of the North, the South, the East, or the West; but is, simply, whether nineteen millions of people shall tamely and ignobly permit five or six millions to overthrow and destroy institutions which are the common property, and have been the common blessings and glory of all. The great thoroughfares of the North, the East, and the West, are luminous with the banners and glistening with the bayonets of citizen soldiers marching to the Capital, or to the other points of rendevouz; but they come in no hostile spirit to the South. *If called to press her soil, they will not ruffle a flower of her gardens, nor a blade of grass of her fields in unkindness. No excesses will mark the footsteps of the armies of the Republic; no institution of the States will be invaded or tampered with, no rights of persons or of property will be violated. The known purposes of the Administration, and the high character of the troops employed, alike guarantee the truthfulness of this statement.* When an insurrection was apprehended a few weeks since in Maryland, the Massachusetts' Regiment at once offered their services to suppress it. These volunteers have been denounced by the Press of the South as "knaves and vagrants," "the dregs and offscourings of the populace," who would "rather filch a handkerchief than fight an enemy in manly combat;" yet we know here that their discipline and bearing are most admirable, and, I presume, it may be safely affirmed, that a larger amount of social position, culture, fortune, and elevation of character, has never been found in so large an army in any age or country. *If they go to the South, it will be as friends and protectors, to relieve the Union sentiment of the seceded States from the cruel domination by which it is oppressed and silenced, to unfurl the Stars and Stripes in the midst of those who long to look upon them, and to restore the flag that bears them to the forts and arsenals from which disloyal hands have torn it.* Their mission will be one of peace, unless wicked and bloodthirsty men shall unsheath the sword across their pathway.

It is in vain for the revolutionists to exclaim that this is *"subjugation."* It is so, precisely in the sense in which you and I and all law-abiding citizens are subjugated. The people of the South are our brethren, and while we obey the laws enacted by our joint authority, and keep a compact to which we all are parties, we only ask that they shall be required to do the same. We believe that their safety demands this; we know that ours does. We impose no burden which we ourselves do not bear; we claim no privilege or blessing which our brethren of the South shall not equally share. Their country is our country, and ours is theirs; and that unity both of country and of government which the providence of God and the compacts of men have created we could not ourselves, without self-immolation, destroy, nor can we permit it to be destroyed by others.

Equally vain is it for them to declare that they only wish "to be let alone," and that, in establishing the independence of the seceded States, they do those which remain in the old Confederacy no harm. The Free States, if allowed the opportunity of doing so, will undoubtedly concede every guarantee needed to afford complete protection to the institutions of the South, and to furnish assurances of her perfect equality in the Union; but all such guarantees and assurances are now openly spurned, and the only Southern right now insisted on is that of dismembering the Republic. It is perfectly certain, that in the attempted exercise of this right, neither States nor statesmen will be "let alone." Should a ruffian meet me

in the streets, and seek, with his axe, to hew an arm and
a leg from my body, I would not the less resist him because, as a dishonoured and helpless trunk, I might per-
chance survive the mutilation. It is easy to perceive what
fatal results to the old Confederacy would follow, should
the blow now struck at its integrity ultimately triumph.
We can well understand what degradation it would bring
to it abroad, and what weakness at home; what exhaus-
tion from incessant war and standing armies, and from
the erection of fortifications along the thousands of miles
of new frontiers; what embarrassments to commerce from
having its natural channels encumbered or cut off; what
elements of disintregation and revolution would be introduced from the pernicious example; and, above all, what
humiliation would cover the whole American people for
having failed in their great mission to demonstrate before
the world the capacity of our race for self-government.

*While a far more fearful responsibility has fallen upon
President Lincoln than upon any of his predecessors, it
must be admitted that he has met it with promptitude and
fearlessness.* CICERO, in one of his orations against
CATALINE, speaking of the credit due himself for having
suppressed the conspiracy of that arch-traitor, said, "If
the glory of him who founded Rome was great, how much
greater should be that of him who had saved it from overthrow, after it had grown to be mistress of the world?" So
may it be said of the glory of that statesman or chieftain
who shall snatch this Republic from the vortex of revolution, now that it has expanded from ocean to ocean,—has
become the admiration of the world, and has rendered the
fountains of the lives of thirty millions of people fountains
of happiness.

B

The vigorous measures adopted for the safety of Washington, and the Government itself, may seem open to criticism, in some of their details, to those who have yet to learn that not only has war, like peace, its laws, but that it has also its privileges and its duties. Whatever of severity, or even of irregularity, may have arisen, will find its justification in the pressure of the terrible necessity under which the Administration has been called to act. When a man feels the poignard of the destroyer at his bosom, he is not likely to consult the law-books as to the mode or measure of his rights of self-defence. What is true of individuals is in this respect equally true of governments. *The man who thinks he has become disloyal because of what the Administration has done, will probably discover, after a close examination, that he was disloyal before.* But for what has been done, Washington might ere this have been a smouldering heap of ruins.

They have noted the course of public affairs to little advantage who suppose that the election of LINCOLN was the real ground of the revolutionary outbreak that has occurred. The roots of the revolution may be traced back for more than a quarter of a century, and an unholy lust for power is the soil out of which it sprang. A prominent member of the band of agitators declared in one of his speeches at Charleston, last November or December, that they had been occupied for thirty years in the work of severing South Carolina from the Union. When General JACKSON crushed nullification, he said it would revive again under the form of the slavery agitation, and we have lived to see his prediction verified. Indeed, that agitation, during the last fifteen or twenty years, has been almost the entire stock in trade of Southern politicians.

The Southern people, known to be as generous in their impulses as they are chivalric, were not wrought into a frenzy of passion by the intemperate words of a few fanatical abolitionists; for these words, if left to themselves, would have fallen to the ground as pebbles into the sea, and would have been heard of no more. But it was the echo of those words, repeated with exaggerations for the thousandth time by Southern politicians, in the halls of Congress, and in the deliberative and popular assemblies, and through the Press of the South, that produced the exasperation which has proved so potent a lever in the hands of the conspirators. The cloud was fully charged, and the juggling revolutionists who held the wires, and could at will direct its lightnings, appeared at Charleston, broke up the Democratic Convention assembled to nominate a candidate for the Presidency, and thus secured the election of Mr. LINCOLN. Having thus rendered this certain, they at once set to work to bring the popular mind of the South to the point of determining in advance that the election of a Republican President would be *per se* cause for a dissolution of the Union. They were but too successful, and to this result the inaction and indecision of the Border States deplorably contributed. When the election of Mr. LINCOLN was announced, there was rejoicing in the streets of Charleston, and doubtless at other points in the South; for it was believed by the conspirators that this had brought a tide in the current of their machinations which would bear them on to victory. The drama of secession was now open, and State after State rapidly rushed out of the Union, and their members withdrew from Congress. The revolution was pressed on with this hot haste in order that no time should be allowed for

reaction in the Northern mind, or for any adjustment of
the Slavery issues by the action of Congress or of the
State Legislatures. Had the Southern members continued in their seats, a satisfactory compromise would, no
doubt, have been arranged and passed before the adjourn-
ment of Congress. As it was, after their retirement, and
after Congress had become Republican, an amendment to
the Constitution was adopted by a two-thirds vote, declaring that Congress should never interfere with Slavery in
the States, and declaring, further, that this amendment
should be irrevocable. Thus we falsified the clamor so
long and so insidiously rung in the ears of the Southern
people, that the abolition of Slavery in the States was the
ultimate aim of the Republican party. But even this
amendment, and all others which may be needed to furnish
the guarantees demanded, are now defeated by the secession of eleven States, which, claiming to be out of the
Union, will refuse to vote upon, and, in effect, will vote
against, any proposals to modify the Federal Constitution.
There are now thirty-four States in the Confederacy,
three-fourths of which, being twenty-six, must concur in
the adoption of any amendment before it can become a
part of the Constitution; but the secession of eleven States
leaves but twenty-three whose vote can possibly be secured,
which is less than the constitutional number.

Thus we have the extraordinary and discreditable spectacle of a revolution made by certain States professedly
on the ground that guarantees for the safety of their
institutions are denied them, and, at the same time, instead of co-operating with their sister States in obtaining
these guarantees, they designedly assume a hostile attitude, and thereby render it constitutionally impossible to

secure them. This profound dissimulation shows that it was not the safety of the South but its severance from the Confederacy, which was sought from the beginning. Cotemporary with, and in some cases preceding, these acts of secession, the greatest outrages were committed upon the Government of the United States by the States engaged in them. Its forts, arsenals, arms, barracks, custom-houses, post-offices, moneys, and, indeed, every species of its property within the limits of these States, were seized and appropriated, down to the very hospital stores for the sick soldiers. More than half a million of dollars was plundered from the mint at New Orleans. United States vessels were received from the defiled hands of their officers in command, and, as if in the hope of consecrating official treachery as one of the public virtues of the age, the surrender of an entire military department by a General, to the keeping of whose honour it had been confided, was deemed worthy of the commendation and thanks of the Conventions of several States. All these lawless proceedings were well understood to have been prompted and directed by men occupying seats in the Capitol, some of whom were frank enough to declare that they could not and would not, though in a minority, live under a Government which they could not control. In this declaration is found the key which unlocks the whole of the complicated machinery of this revolution. The profligate ambition of public men in all ages and lands has been the rock on which republics have been split. Such men have arisen in our midst—men who, because unable permanently to grasp the helm of the ship, are willing to destroy it in the hope to command some one of the rafts that may float away from the wreck.

B*

The effect is to degrade us to a level with the military bandits of Mexico and South America, who, when beaten at an election, fly to arms, and seek to master by the sword what they have been unable to control by the ballot-box.

The atrocious acts enumerated were acts of war, and might all have been treated as such by the late Administration; but the President patriotically cultivated peace—how anxiously and how patiently the country well knows. *While, however, the revolutionary leaders greeted him with all hails to his face, they did not the less diligently continue to whet their swords behind his back. Immense military preparations were made, so that when the moment for striking at the Government of the United States arrived, the revolutionary States leaped into the contest clad in full armour.*

As if nothing should be wanting to darken this page of history, the seceded States have already entered upon the work of confiscating the debts due from their citizens to the North and Northwest. The millions thus gained will doubtless prove a pleasant substitute for those guarantees now so scornfully rejected. To these confiscations will probably succeed soon those of lands and negroes owned by citizens of loyal States; and, indeed, the apprehension of this step is already sadly disturbing the fidelity of non-resident proprietors. Fortunately, however, infirmity of faith, springing from such a cause, is not likely to be contagious. *The war begun is being prosecuted by the Confederate States in a temper as fierce and unsparing as that which characterizes conflicts between the most hostile nations. Letters of marque and reprisal are being granted* to all who seek them, so that our coasts will soon swarm with these piratical cruisers, as the President has properly denounced them. Every buccaneer who desires to rob American commerce upon the ocean, can, for the asking, obtain a warrant to do so, in the name of the new republic. To crown all, large bodies of Indians have been mustered into the service of the revolutionary States, and are now conspicuous in the ranks of the Southern army. A leading North Carolina journal, noting their stalwart frames and unerring markmanship, observes, with an exultation positively fiendish, that they are armed, not only with the rifle, but also with *the scalping-knife and tomahawk.*

Is Kentucky willing to link her name in history with the excesses and crimes which have sullied this revolution at every step of its progress? Can she soil her pure hands with its booty? She possesses the noblest heritage that God has granted to his children; is she prepared to barter it away for that miserable mess of pottage which the gratification of the unholy ambition of her public men would bring to her lips? Can she, without laying her face in the very dust for shame, become a participant in the spoliation of the commerce of her neighbours and friends, by contributing her star, hitherto so stainless in its glory, to light the corsair on his way? Has the war-whoop, which used to startle the sleep of our frontiers, so died away in her ears that she is willing to take the red-handed savage to her bosom as the champion of her rights and the representative of her spirit? Must she not first forget her own heroic sons who perished, butchered and scalped, upon the disastrous field of Raisin?

The object of the revolution, as avowed by all who are pressing it forward, is the permanent dismemberment of the

Confederacy. The dream of reconstruction—used during the last winter as a lure to draw the hesitating or the hopeful into the movement—has been formally abandoned. If Kentucky separates herself from the Union, it must be upon the basis that the separation is to be final and eternal. Is there aught in the organization or administration of the Government of the United States to justify, on her part, an act so solemn and so perilous? Could the wisest of her lawyers, if called upon, find material for an indictment in any or in all the pages of the history of the Republic? Could the most leprous-lipped of its calumniators point to a single State or Territory, or community or citizen, that it has wronged or oppressed? It would be impossible. *So far as the Slave States are concerned, their protection has been complete, and if it has not been, it has been the fault of their statesmen, who have had the control of the Government since its foundation.*

The census returns show that during the year 1860 the Fugitive Slave Law was executed more faithfully and successfully than it had been during the preceding ten years. Since the installation of President LINCOLN, not a case has arisen in which the fugitive has not been returned, and that, too, without any opposition from the people. Indeed, the fidelity with which it was understood to be the policy of the Administration to enforce the provisions of this law, has caused a perfect panic among the runaway slaves in the Free States, and they have been escaping in multitudes to Canada, unpursued and unreclaimed by their masters. Is there found in this, reason for a dissolution of the Union?

That the Slave States are not recognized as equals in

the Confederacy, has for several years been the cry of
demagogues and conspirators. But what is the truth?
Not only according to the theory, but the actual practice
of the Government, the Slave States have ever been, and
still are, in all respects, the peers of the Free. Of the
fourteen Presidents who have been elected, seven were
citizens of Slave States, and of the seven remaining, three
represented Southern principles, and received the votes
of the Southern people; so that, in our whole history,
but four Presidents have been chosen who can be claimed
as the special champions of the policy and principles of
the Free States, and even these so only in a modified
sense. Does this look as if the South had ever been de-
prived of her equal share of the honours and powers of the
Government? The Supreme Court has decided that the
citizens of the Slave States can, at will, take their slaves
into all the Territories of the United States; and this
decision, which has never been resisted or interfered with
in a single case, is the law of the land, and the whole
power of the Government is pledged to enforce it. That
it will be loyally enforced by the present Administration
I entertain no doubt. A Republican Congress, at the
late session, organized three new Territories, and in the
organic law of neither was there introduced, or attempted
to be introduced, the slightest restriction upon the rights
of the Southern emigrant to bring his slaves with him.
At this moment, therefore, and I state it without qualifica-
tion, there is not a Territory belonging to the United
States into which the Southern people may not introduce
their slaves at pleasure, and enjoy there complete protection. Kentucky should consider this great and undeniable
fact, before which all the frothy rant of demagogues and

disunionists must disappear as a bank of fog before the wind. But were it otherwise, and did a defect exist in our organic law, or in the practical administration of the Government, in reference to the rights of Southern slave-holders in the Territories, still the question would be a mere abstraction, since the laws of climate forbid the establishment of slavery in such a latitude; and to destroy such institutions as ours for such a cause, instead of patiently trying to remove it, would be a little short of national insanity. It would be to burn the house down over our heads merely because there is a leak in the roof; to scuttle the ship in mid-ocean merely because there is a difference of opinion among the crew as to the point of the compass to which the vessel should be steered; it would be, in fact, to apply the knife to the throat instead of to the cancer of the patient.

But what remains? Though, say the Disunionists, the Fugitive Slave Law is honestly enforced, and though, under the shelter of the Supreme Court, we can take our slaves into the Territories, yet the Northern people will persist in discussing the institution of Slavery, and there-fore we will break up the Government. It is true that Slavery has been very intemperately discussed in the North, and it is equally true that until we have an Asiatic despotism, crushing out all freedom of speech and of the press, this discussion will probably continue. In this age and country all institutions, human and divine, are dis-cussed, and so they ought to be; and all that cannot bear discussion must go to the wall, where they ought to go. It is not pretended, however, that the discussion of Slavery, which has been continued in our country for more than forty years, has in any manner disturbed or weakened the foundation of the institution. On the contrary, we learn from the press of the seceded States that their slaves were never more tranquil or obedient. There are zealots—happily few in number—both North and South, whose language upon this question is alike extravagant and alike deserving our condemnation. Those who assert that Slavery should be extirpated by the sword, and those who maintain that the great mission of the white man upon earth is to enslave the black, are not far apart in the folly and atrocity of their sentiments.

Before proceeding further, Kentucky should measure well the depth of the gulf she is approaching, and look well to the feet of her guides. Before forsaking a Union in which her people have enjoyed such uninterrupted and such boundless prosperity, she should ask herself, not once, but many times, Why do I go, and where am I going? In view of what has been said, it would be difficult to answer the first branch of the inquiry, but to answer the second part is patent to all, as are the consequences which would follow the movement. In giving her great material and moral resources to the support of the Southern Confederacy, Kentucky might prolong the desolating struggle that rebellious States are making to overthrow a Government which they have only known in its blessings; but the triumph of the Government would nevertheless be certain in the end. *She would abandon a Government strong and able to protect her for one that is weak, and that contains, in the very elements of its life, the seeds of distraction and early dissolution. She would adopt, as the law of her existence, the right of secession— a right which has no foundation in jurisprudence, or logic, or in our political history: which Madison, the father of*

*the Federal Constitution, denounced: which has been de-
nounced by most of the States and prominent statesmen
now insisting upon its exercise; which, in introducing a
principle of indefinite disintegration, cuts up all confederate governments by the roots, and gives them over a prey
to the caprices, and passions, and transient interests of
their members, as autumnal leaves are given to the winds
which blow upon them.* In 1814, the *Richmond Enquirer*,
then, as now, the organ of public opinion in the South,
pronounced secession to be treason, and nothing else, and
such was then the doctrine of Southern statesmen. What
was true then is equally true now. The prevalence of
this pernicious heresy is mainly the fruit of that farce
called "State Rights," which demagogues have been so
long playing under tragic mask, and which has done more
than all things else to unsettle the foundations of the
Republic, by estranging the people from the Federal
Government, as one to be distrusted and resisted, instead
of being, what it is, emphatically their own creation, at
all times obedient to their will, and in its ministrations
the grandest reflex of the greatness and beneficence of
popular power that has ever ennobled the history of our
race. Said Mr. CLAY: "I owe a supreme allegiance to
the General Government, and to my State a subordinate
one." And this terse language disposes of the whole
controversy which has arisen out of the secession movement in regard to the allegiance of the citizen. As the
power of the States and Federal Government are in
perfect harmony with each other, so there can be no conflict between the allegiance due to them; each, while
acting within the sphere of its constitutional authority, is
entitled to be obeyed; but when a State, throwing off all

constitutional restraints, seeks to destroy the General Government, to say that its citizens are bound to follow it in this career of crime, and discard the supreme allegience they owe to the Government assailed, is one of the shallowest and most dangerous fallacies that has ever gained credence among men.

Kentucky, occupying a central position in the Union, is now protected from the scourge of foreign war, however much its ravages may waste the towns and cities upon our coasts, or the commerce upon our seas; but as a member of the Southern Confederacy, she would be a frontier State, and necessarily the victim of those border feuds and conflicts which have become proverbial in history alike for their fierceness and frequency. The people of the South now sleep quietly in their beds, while there is not a home in infatuated and misguided Virginia that is not filled with the alarms and oppressed by the terrors of war. In the fate of the ancient Commonwealth, dragged to the altar of sacrifice by those who should have stood between her bosom and every foe, Kentucky may read her own. *No wonder, therefore, that she has been so coaxingly besought to unite her fortunes with those of the South, and to lay down the bodies of her chivalric sons as a breastwork, behind which the Southern people may be sheltered.* Even as attached to the Southern Confederacy, she would be weak for all the purposes of self-protection, as compared with her present position. But amid the mutations incident to such a helpless and disintegrating league, Kentucky would probably soon find herself adhering to a mere fragment of the Confederacy, or it may be standing entirely alone, in the presence of tiers of Free States, with populations exceeding, by many millions, her own. Feeble States,

C

thus separated from powerful and warlike neighbours by ideal boundaries, or by fears as easily traversed as rivulets, are as insects that feed upon the lion's lip—liable at every moment to be crushed. The recorded doom of multitudes of such, has left us a warning too solemn and impressive to be disregarded.

Kentucky now scarcely feels the contribution she makes to support the Government of the United States, but as a member of the Southern Confederacy, of whose policy free trade will be a cardinal principle, she will be burdened with direct taxation to the amount of double, or, it may be, triple or quadruple that which she now pays into her own treasury. Superadded to this will be required from her her share of those vast outlays necessary for the creation of a navy, the erection of forts and custom-houses along a frontier of several thousand miles; and for the maintenance of that large standing army which will be indispensable at once for her safety, and for imparting to the new government that strong military character which, it has been openly avowed, the peculiar institutions of the South will inexorably demand.

Kentucky now enjoys for her peculiar institution the protection of the Fugitive Slave law, loyally enforced by the Government, and it is this law, effective in its power of recapture, but infinitely more potent in its moral agency in preventing the escape of slaves, that alone saves that institution in the Border States from utter extinction. She cannot carry this law with her into the new Confederacy. She will, virtually, have Canada brought to her doors in the form of Free States, whose population, relieved of all moral and constitutional obligations to deliver up fugitive slaves, will stand, with open arms, inviting and welcoming them, and defending them, if need be, at the point of the bayonet. Under such influences, slavery will perish rapidly away in Kentucky, as a ball of snow would melt in a summer's sun.

Kentucky, in her soul, abhors the African slave-trade, and turns away with unspeakable horror and loathing from the red altars of King Dahomey. *But although this traffic has been temporarily interdicted by the seceded States, it is well understood that this step has been taken as a mere measure of policy for the purpose of impressing the Border States, and of conciliating the European powers. The ultimate legalization of this trade, by a Republic professing to be based upon African servitude, must follow as certainly as does the conclusion from the premises of a mathematical proposition.* Is Kentucky prepared to see the hand upon the dial-plate of her civilization rudely thrust back a century, and to stand before the world the confessed champion of the African Slave-hunter? Is she, with her unsullied fame, ready to become a pander to the rapacity of the African Slave-trader, who burdens the very winds of the sea with the moans of the wretched captives whose limbs he has loaded with chains, and whose hearts he has broken? I do not, I cannot, believe it.

For this catalogue of what Kentucky must suffer in abandoning her present honoured and secure position, and becoming a member of the Southern Confederacy, what will be her indemnity? Nothing, absolutely nothing. The ill-woven ambition of some of her sons may possibly reach the Presidency of the new Republic; that is all. Alas! alas! for that dream of the Presidency of a Southern Republic, which has disturbed so many pillows in the South, and perhaps some in the West, also, and whose lurid light, like a demon's torch, is leading a nation to perdition!

The clamour that in insisting upon the South obeying the laws, the great principle that all popular governments rest upon the consent of the governed is violated, should not receive a moment's consideration. Popular government does, indeed, rest upon the consent of the governed, but it is upon the consent, *not of all, but of a majority of the governed.* Criminals are every day punished, and made to obey the laws, certainly against their will, and no man supposes that the principle referred to is thereby invaded. A bill passed by the Legislature, by the majority of a single vote only, though the constituents of all who voted against it, should be in fact, as they are held to be in theory, opposed to its provisions, still is not the less operative as a law, and no right of self-government is thereby trampled upon. The clamour alluded to assumes that the States are separate and independent governments, and that laws enacted under the authority of all may be resisted and repealed at the pleasure of each. The people of the United States, so far as the powers of the General Government are concerned, are a unit, and laws passed by a majority of all are binding upon all. The laws and Constitution, however, which the South now resists, have been adopted by her sanction, and the right she now claims is that of a feeble minority to repeal what a majority has adopted. Nothing could be more fallacious.

Civil war, under all circumstances, is a terrible

calamity, and yet, from the selfish ambition and wickedness of men, the best governments have not been able to escape it. In regarding that which has been forced upon the Government of the United States, Kentucky should not look so much at the means which may be necessarily employed in its prosecution, as at the machinations by which this national tragedy has been brought upon us. When I look upon this bright land, a few months since so prosperous, so tranquil, and so free, and now behold it desolated by war, and the firesides of its thirty millions of people darkened, and their bosoms wrung with anguish, and know, as I do, that all this is the work of a score or two of men, who, over all this national ruin and despair, are preparing to carve with the sword their way to seats of permanent power, I cannot but feel that they are accumulating upon their soil an amount of guilt hardly equalled in all the atrocities of treason and of homicide that have degraded the annals of our race from the foundations of the world. *Kentucky may rest well assured that this conflict, which is one of self-defence, will be pursued on the part of the Government in the paternal spirit in which a father seeks to reclaim his erring offspring. No conquest, no effusion of blood is sought. In sorrow, not in anger, the prayer of all is, that the end may be reached without loss of life or waste of property.* Among the most powerful instrumentalities relied on for re-establishing the authority of the Government, is that of the Union sentiment of the South, sustained by a liberated press. It is now trodden to the earth under a reign of terrorism which has no parallel but in the worst days of the French Revolution. The presence of the Govern-
c*

ment will enable it to rebound and look its oppressors in
the face. At present we are assured that in the seceded
States no man expresses an opinion opposed to the revolution but at the hazard of his life and property. The
only light which is admitted into political discussion is
that which flashes from the sword or gleams from glistening bayonets. A few days since, one of the United
States Senators from Virginia published a manifesto, in
which he announces, with oracular solemnity and severity,
that all citizens who would not vote for secession, but
were in favour of the Union—not, should, or ought to—
but "MUST leave the State." These words have in them
decidedly the crack of the overseer's whip. The Senator
evidently treats Virginia as a great negro quarter, in
which the lash is the appropriate emblem of authority,
and the only argument he will condescend to use. However the freemen of other parts of the State may abase
themselves under the exercise of this insolent and pro-
scriptive tyranny, should the Senator, with his scourge of
slaves, endeavour to drive the people of Western Virginia
from their homes, I will only say, in the language of the
narrative of Gilpin's ride,

"May I be there to see!"

It would certainly prove a deeply interesting spectacle.

It is true that before this deliverance of the popular
mind of the South from the threatenings and alarm which
have subdued it can be accomplished, the remorseless
agitators who have made this revolution, and now hold its
reins, must be discarded alike from the public confidence
and the public service. The country in its agony is feel-

ing their power, and we well understand how difficult will
be the task of overthrowing the ascendancy they have
secured. But the Union men of the South—believed to
be in the majority in every seceded State, except, perhaps,
South Carolina—aided by the presence of the Government, will be fully equal to the emergency. Let these
agitators perish, politically, if need be, by scores,

"A breath can unmake them as a breath has made;"

but destroy this Republic, and

"Where is that Promethean heat
That can its light relume?"

Once entombed, when will the Angel of the Resurrec-
tion descend to the portals of its sepulchre? There is
not a voice which comes to us from the cemetery of nations
that does not answer: "Never, never!" Amid the tor-
ments of perturbed existence, we may have glimpses of
rest and of freedom, as the maniac has glimpses of reason
between the paroxysms of his madness, but we shall attain
to neither national dignity nor national repose. We
shall be a mass of jarring, warring, fragmentary States,
enfeebled and demoralized, without power at home, or
respectability abroad, and, like the republics of Mexico
and South America, we will drift away on a shoreless and
ensanguined sea of civil commotion, from which, if the
teachings of history are to be trusted, we shall finally be
rescued by the iron hand of some military wrecker, who
will coin the shattered elements of our greatness and of
our strength in a diadem and a throne. Said M. FOULD,
the great French statesman, to an American citizen, a
few weeks since: "Your Republic is dead, and it is pro-

bably the last the world will ever see. You will have a reign of terrorism, and after that two or three monarchies." All this may be verified, should this revolution succeed.

Let us then twine each thread of the glorious tissue of our country's flag about our heart-strings, and looking upon our homes and catching the spirit that breathes upon us from the battle-fields of our fathers, let us resolve, that come weal or woe, we will in life and in death, now and for ever, stand by the Stars and the Stripes. They have floated over our cradles, let it be our prayer and our struggle that they shall float over our graves. They have been unfurled from the snows of Canada to the plains of New Orleans, and to the halls of the Montezumas, and amid the solitudes of every sea; and everywhere, as the luminous symbol of resistless and beneficent power, they have led the brave and the free to victory and to glory. It has been my fortune to look upon this flag in foreign lands and amid the gloom of an oriental despotism, and right well do I know, by contrast, how bright are its stars, and how sublime are its inspirations! If this banner, the emblem for us of all that is grand in human history, and of all that is transporting in human hope, is to be sacrificed on the altars of a Satanic ambition, and thus disappear for ever amid the night and tempest of revolution, then will I feel—and who shall estimate the desolation of that feeling?—that the sun has indeed been stricken from the sky of our lives, and that henceforth we shall be but wanderers and outcasts, with nought but the bread of sorrow and of penury for our lips, and with hands ever outstretched in feebleness and supplication, on which, in any hour, a military tyrant may rivet the fetters of a despairing bondage. May God in his infinite mercy save you and me, and the land we so much love, from the doom of such a degradation.

No contest so momentous as this has arisen in human history, for, amid all the conflicts of men and of nations, the life of no such government as ours has ever been at stake. Our fathers won our Independence by the blood and sacrifices of a seven years' war, and we have maintained it against the assaults of the greatest Power upon the earth; and the question now is, whether we are to perish by our own hands, and have the epitaph of suicide written upon our tomb? The ordeal through which we are passing must involve immense suffering and losses for us all, but the expenditure of not merely hundreds of millions, but of billions of treasure, will be well made, if the result shall be the preservation of our institutions.

Could my voice reach every dwelling in Kentucky, I would implore its inmates—if they would not have the rivers of their prosperity shrink away, as do unfed streams beneath the summer heats—to rouse themselves from their lethargy, and fly to the rescue of their country, before it is everlastingly too late. Man should appeal to man, and neighbourhood to neighbourhood, until the electric fires of patriotism shall flash from heart to heart in one unbroken current throughout the land. It is a time in which the work-shop, the office, the counting-house, and the field, may well be abandoned for the solemn duty that is upon us, for all these toils will but bring treasure, not for ourselves, but for the spoiler, if this revolution is not arrested.

We are all, with our every earthly interest, embarked in mid ocean on the same common deck. The howl of the storm is in our ears, and "the lightning's red glare is painting hell on the sky ;" and while the noble ship pitches and rolls under the lashings of the waves, the cry is heard that she has sprung a leak at many points, and that the rushing waters are mounting rapidly in the hold. The *man who, in such an hour, will not work at the pumps, is either a maniac or a monster.*

Sincerely yours,

JOSEPH HOLT.

LETTER FROM HON. EDWARD EVERETT.

The following private letter was written, without any thought of publication, to a correspondent in Virginia.

BOSTON, *May* 15, 1861.

MY DEAR MR. ——.

Your letter of the 9th reached me yesterday. I read it with mingled feelings; gratified that your friendly regard had as yet survived the shock of the times, and deeply grieved at the different view we take of the existing crisis.

It is well known to you that I sustained the South, at the almost total sacrifice of influence and favour at home, as long as I thought she was pursuing constitutional objects. This I did, although the South had placed the conservative North in a false and indefensible position, by the repeal of the Missouri Compromise, and the persevering attempts to force slavery into the Territory of Kansas, by surprise, fraud and violence, against the known wish of an overwhelming majority of the people. I pursued this course for the sake of strengthening the hands of patriotic Union men at the South; *although I was well aware, partly from facts within my personal knowledge, that leading Southern politicians had for thirty years been resolved to break up the Union, as soon*

as they ceased to control the United States Government,
and that the slavery question was but a pretext for keeping up agitation and rallying the South.

Notwithstanding this state of things, and the wholly
unwarrantable manner in which the policy of secession
was initiated by South Carolina and followed up by the
other cotton States, and in spite of the seizure of the
public establishments and the public property—which,
in the absence of any joint act of partition, was sheer
plunder—it was my opinion that, if they would abstain
from further aggression, and were determined to separate,
we had better part in peace. But the wanton attack on
Fort Sumter (which took place, not from any military
necessity, for what harm was a single company, cooped
up in Charleston harbour, able to do to South Carolina?
but for the avowed purpose of "stirring the blood" of
the South, and thus bringing in the border States), and
the subsequent proceedings at Montgomery, have wholly
changed the state of affairs. The South has levied an
unprovoked war against the Government of the United
States, the mildest and most beneficent in the world, and
has made it the duty of every good citizen to rally to its
support.

I perceive that my having publicly expressed that
sentiment, and contributed my mite toward the regiment
of Mr. Webster (who inherits the conservative opinions
of his illustrious father), has caused surprise on the part
of some of my Southern friends—yourself among the most
valued of them—as if my so doing was inconsistent with
the friendly feelings I have ever cherished toward the
South. But these friends forget that as early as the

12th of April, that is, before the proclamation of President Lincoln, the Secretary of War at Montgomery had threatened that by the 1st of May, the Confederate flag should float over the Capitol at Washington, and in due time our Faneuil Hall. When General Beauregard proceeds to execute this threat, his red-hot cannon balls and shells will not spare the roof that shelters my daughter and four little children at Washington, nor my own roof in Boston. Must I, because I have been the steady friend of the South, sit still while he is battering my house about my ears?

I certainly deprecated the choice of a President exclusively by the electoral vote of one section of the country, though consenting with the greatest reluctance to be myself upon one of the opposing tickets. It was, however, fully in the power of the South to have produced a different result. *But the disunionists were determined to have their own candidate, though mistaken, I trust, in the belief that he shared their disloyal views. I make this charge against them without scruple, justified by subsequent events, as well as by the language of the entire Union press at the South during the canvass.*

After the election was decided, the disunionists would not wait for *overt acts*, because they knew none could or would be committed. They knew that there was an anti-Republican majority in the Senate, and that there would be one in the present House. *They "precipitated" the rupture of the Union, because they knew that if they waited, even the pretext for it would fail.*

After the cotton States had seceded, and although that circumstance greatly increased the difficulty of compro-

D

misc, measures were nevertheless adopted or proposed in Congress, which must have removed all sincere alarm on the part of the South, that their Constitutional rights were threatened. The accredited leaders of the Republican party, including the President elect, uniformly pledged themselves to that effect. The two Houses by a constitutional majority pledged them in like manner against any future amendment of the Constitution violating the rights of the South. A member from Massachusetts, (Mr. Adams,) possessing the entire confidence of the incoming Administration, proposed to admit New Mexico as a State, and three new Territories were organized without any anti-slavery restriction. While this was done in Congress, the States repealed or modified the laws throwing obstacles in the way of recovering fugitive slaves—laws which have never been of any practical injury to the cotton States. These conciliatory demonstrations had no effect in staying the progress of secession, *because the leaders of that revolution were determined not to be satisfied*, and to maintain their policy, which, in the light of the Constitution, is simple rebellion and treason, they have appealed to the sword.

You say that the South desires nothing but peace, and ask whether the North will not "let you alone." But, my good friend, the South demands a great deal more than "peace." She claims the capital of the country, although she has but a third of its population. She claims the control of the outlet of Chesapeake Bay and its tributaries; the right to command the most direct route (the Baltimore and Ohio Railroad) to the Atlantic from Ohio, Indiana, and Illinois—States whose population amounts to five and a half millions; the right to dragoon the State of Maryland and the Western part of your own State, with Kentucky, Missouri, and Tennessee, into joining the Southern Confederacy; the right to occupy the fortresses which protect the trade of the Gulf of Mexico; the right to shut up the outlet of the Ohio, Mississippi, and the Missouri; and, finally, she claims the right for any State, that chooses to pass a law to that effect, to break up the Union. In enforcing these unconstitutional, monstrous, and unheard of usurpations, she asks to be "let alone;" and when the Government of the United States, in obedience to the solemn oaths of its members, (from which the leaders of the revolt dispense themselves,) takes measures to defend itself, the capital of the Union, the public establishments and the rights of the whole people against this invasion, long premeditated by ambitious and disappointed politicians, (for Mr. A. H. Stephens truly declares that to be "the source of a great part of our troubles,") she exclaims that the North seeks to "subjugate the South."

I cannot describe to you, my dear friend, the sorrow caused me by this state of things. Circumstances, as you well knew, had led me to form personal friendly relations at the South, more extensively than most Northern men, and the support given, especially in the Border States, to the ticket on which my name was borne at the late election, filled me with gratitude. If the sacrifice of all I have, could have averted the present disastrous struggle, I could have made it willingly, joyously. But I pray you, believe me that I speak not only my own conviction, but that of the entire North, when I say that we feel that the conflict has been forced upon us, to gratify the aspirations of ambitious men; that it is our duty to ourselves, to our children, and to the whole people, to sustain the Government; and that it is, if possible, more the interest of the South than of the North, that this attempt to break up the Union should fail.

I remain, my dear Mr.———,

Sorrowfully and sincerely yours,

EDWARD EVERETT.

LETTER FROM COMMODORE STEWART.

BORDENTOWN, *May*, 4, 1861.

MY DEAR SIR:

Agreeably to your request I now furnish you with the reminiscences of a conversation which passed between Mr. John C. Calhoun and myself, in the latter part of December, 1812, after the declaration of war by the Congress of the United States against Great Britain, on the 18th of June previous.

On the assembling of Congress, in the early part of December, I found that an important portion of the leading Democratic members of Congress had taken up their quarters at Mrs. Bushby's boarding-house; amongst whom was Mr. Calhoun—a new member from South Carolina—and I believe this was his first appearance in the House of Representatives. In consequence of this I took Lieutenant Ridgley, my confidential officer and the first Lieutenant of the frigate Constellation, of which vessel I then held the command, and was preparing for sea at the Washington navy yard—left our lodgings at Strothers' and obtained board at Mrs. Bushby's with them. Ridgley was a witty and able talker, who could aid me in demonstrating the necessity for, and the high policy of, a formidable naval force, wherewith to carry on the war with

D*

England, which I considered could only be done with effect through her being victoriously struck at on an element over which she deemed herself sole mistress. This appeared to me to constitute her most tender point.

By this movement I found myself judiciously located to enable me to urge upon Congress any patriotic measures which seemed best calculated to meet and discomfit the self-sufficiency and arrogance of our oppressive enemy.

Mr. Calhoun's age, I thought, approximated my own, which was then thirty-four, and he being a man of the highest order of talent, and representing a State in our Union which scarce ever permitted themselves to be represented by inferior ability in the national councils, I could not have commenced my object with one more fitted for the purpose I had in view. He was also a high-minded and honourable man, kind and friendly, as well as open and confiding to those he deemed worthy. We soon formed an intimacy, and I frequently had long conversations with him on the war, the subjects relating thereto, and matters growing out of its existence—the navy being the most prominent—the gunboats, the merchants, bonds, then on the tapis in Congress, and others of political or minor interest. One evening I struck on the divided views of our sectional interests—of the war—stated to him that the opposite feelings on this subject had puzzled me exceedingly, and asked him how it was that the planting States were so strongly and so decidedly in favour of the war, while the commercial States were so much opposed to it? With this latter section of our country it seemed to me that the punishment of England, through the medium of war, ought to meet their highest approbation, and call for their greatest efforts, as they were the greatest sufferers through her instrumentality and power over our commercial affairs since 1792, which were so arrogantly urged by plunder and impressment on the highway of. nations, while the Southern portion of the Union had felt but little in comparison. I observed with great simplicity: "You in the South and Southwest are decidedly the aristocratic portion of this Union; you are so in holding persons in perpetuity in slavery; you are so in every domestic quality; so in every habit of your lives, living and actions; so in habits, customs, intercourse and manners; you neither work with your hands, head, nor any machinery, but live and have your living not in accordance with the will of your Creator, but by the sweat of slavery, and yet you assume all the attributes, professions and advantages of Democracy." Mr. Calhoun replied: "I see you speak through the head of a young statesman, and from the heart of a patriot, but you lose sight of the politician and the sectional policy of the people. I admit your conclusions in respect to us Southrons; that we are essentially aristocratic, I cannot deny, but we can and do yield much to Democracy. This is our sectional policy; we are from necessity thrown upon, and solemnly wedded to, that party, however it may occasionally clash with our feelings, for the conservator of our interests. It is through our affiliation with that party in the Middle and Western States we control, under the Constitution, the governing of these United States; but when we cease thus to control this nation through a disjointed Democracy, or any material obstacle in that party which shall tend to throw us out of that rule and control, we shall then resort to the dissolution of the Union. The compromises in the Constitution, under the then circumstances, were sufficient for our fathers, but under the altered condition of our country from that period, leave to the South no resource but dissolution; for no amendments to the Constitution could be reached through a Convention of the people and their three-fourths rule." I laughed incredulously, and said: "Well, Mr. Calhoun, ere such can take place you and I will have been so long *non est* that we can now laugh at its possibility, and leave it with complacency to our children's children, who will then have the watch on deck."

Alas! my dear sir, how entirely were the views of that " young headed statesman" circumscribed by the patriotic feelings of his heart. What he then thought an impossibility for human hands to effect, for ages on ages to come, he now sees verified to the letter, as predicted by that far-seeing statesman, JOHN C. CALHOUN. Even this noble Republic is disrupted, its Constitution rent into shreds and tatters by party follies and the wickedness of its people's selfishness. Had they but inherited a moiety of the virtues of their fathers, who bled and impoverished themselves through a long and bloody war to establish the independence and liberty, welfare and happiness of their posterity for all time to come; had they worshipped the true and living God, instead of the "almighty dollar," they would not now have beheld the millions of patriots arming for the strife, against traitors to their country, to the Constitution and the laws, once more to baptize in blood, for liberty's sake, the blessings which rational liberty accords under our Union. Had a prophet arisen in 1812, and predicted as JOHN C. CALHOUN did, nothing short of Divine inspiration could have given credence to his foreshadowings. Alas! I have lived to see its accomplishment. He has gone to the tomb of his fathers, the pride of his section, honoured for his talents and for his efforts in council, while your humble servant still lingers on the brink, under the national anathema of degradation —as a reward for many years of faithful services—which degradation was accorded him simultaneously with his reaching the head of the service to which his whole life had been devoted. You will see, my dear sir, I have no disposition to "bury my light under a bushel," but will ever be ready to accord justice when justice is due. Thus in death we show the ruling passion stronger than in life; and as it is with individuals so it is with nations, the blackest spot found in the heart is ingratitude.

Accept my assurances of regard and respect.

CHARLES STEWART.

GEO. W. CHILDS, Esq., Philad.

PAMPHLETS ON THE CRISIS.

THE CAUSES OF THE AMERICAN CIVIL WAR. A Letter to the *London Times*. By John Lothrop Motley, LL.D., author of "The Rise of the Dutch Republic." Price 10 cts. Per dozen $1.00.

LETTERS OF THE HON. JOSEPH HOLT, THE HON. EDWARD EVERETT, AND COMMODORE CHARLES STEWART, ON THE PRESENT CRISIS. Price 15 cts., or eight copies for $1.00.

THE SCRIPTURE DOCTRINE OF CIVIL GOVERNMENT APPLIED TO THE PRESENT CRISIS. A Discourse delivered in the Westminster Presbyterian Church. By the Rev. Robert Watts. Price 10 cts. Per dozen $1.00.

AMERICAN PATRIOTISM. A Sermon. By the Rev. Charles Wadsworth, D.D. Price 15 cts.

THE CHRISTIAN SOLDIER. A Sermon. By the Rev. Charles Wadsworth, D.D. Price 15 cts.

THE STATE OF THE COUNTRY. Reprinted from the *Princeton Review*. By Rev. Charles Hodge, D.D. Price 6 cts.

A second Article from the *Princeton Review*. By Rev. Dr. Hodge. Price 75 cts.

OUR COUNTRY; ITS PERILS AND ITS DELIVERANCE. By Rev. Robt. J. Breckinridge, D.D. Price 15 cts., or eight copies for $1.00.

DANVILLE QUARTERLY REVIEW FOR JUNE. Containing a Second Article from Rev. Dr. Robert J. Breckinridge on the Crisis. Price 75 cts.

THE REBELLION RECORD; a Diary of the Southern Conspiracy and War against the United States. To be published monthly. Part I. With a portrait of Gen. Scott and a fine Map. Price 50 cts.

Part II. REBELLION RECORD. Containing Portraits of Fremont, Ellsworth, and Jeff. Davis. Price 50 cts.

Any of the above sent by mail, post-paid, on receipt of the price.

For sale by
WILLIAM S. & ALFRED MARTIEN,
606 Chestnut Street, Philadelphia.

MAPS OF THE SEAT OF WAR.

I.

500 *Miles Around the City of Washington*, showing the *Seat of War in the East*, with list of Forts, Military Stations, Table of ·Population, Areas, etc , and an enlarged MILITARY MAP of the country between New York, Washington, and Wheeling—the scene of the present active military operations.

One large sheet, 33 by 23 inches. Price, in sheets, coloured, 25 cts.; in neat pocket cases, 38 cts.

II.

500 *Miles around Cairo*, showing the *Seat of War in the West*, with list of Forts and Military Stations, Distances on Rivers to and from Cairo, etc., and a detailed Map of the Ohio and Mississippi rivers, showing every steamboat landing.

One large sheet, 33 by 23 inches. Price, in sheets, coloured, 25 cts.; in neat pocket cases, 38 cts.

These sheets are the largest and cheapest, the most reliable in information and beautiful in execution, that have yet been issued, and are prepared on an entirely novel plan.

III.

Map of the United States and Territories east of the Rocky Mountains, showing the Military Posts, Ports of Entry, &c. With an enlarged View of the Seat of War, the Coast of South Carolina, and of Fort Pickens, and the Shores of the Gulf of Mexico. Price, coloured, 50 cts.

IV.

Bird's-Eye View of Virginia, Delaware, Maryland, and the District of Columbia. Size, 30 by 36 inches. Price, $1 00.

This is a most carefully and beautifully prepared Map, conveying, at a glance, a correct and comprehensive view of all the leading points of interest, blockading fleets, &c.

For sale by

WILLIAM S. & ALFRED MARTIEN,

606 Chestnut Street, Philadelphia.

www.ingramcontent.com/pod-product-compliance
Lightning Source LLC
Chambersburg PA
CBHW032121080426
42733CB00008B/1008